MAP MY AREA

MAPPING MY WORLD

©2018
Book Life
King's Lynn
Norfolk PE30 4LS

ISBN: 978-1-78637-320-5

Written by:
Harriet Brundle

Edited by:
Kirsty Holmes

Designed by:
Matt Rumbelow

A catalogue record for this book
is available from the British Library.

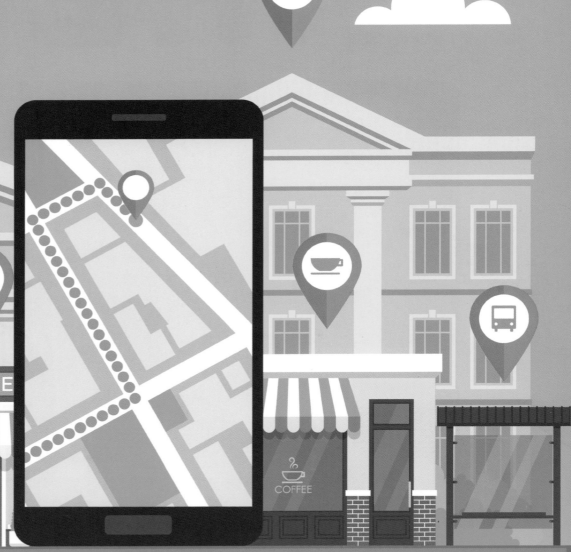

CONTENTS

Words that look like this can be found in the glossary on page 24.

WHAT IS A MAP?

A map is a picture that gives us information about an area. Maps can show us lots of different things, such as roads, population or weather.

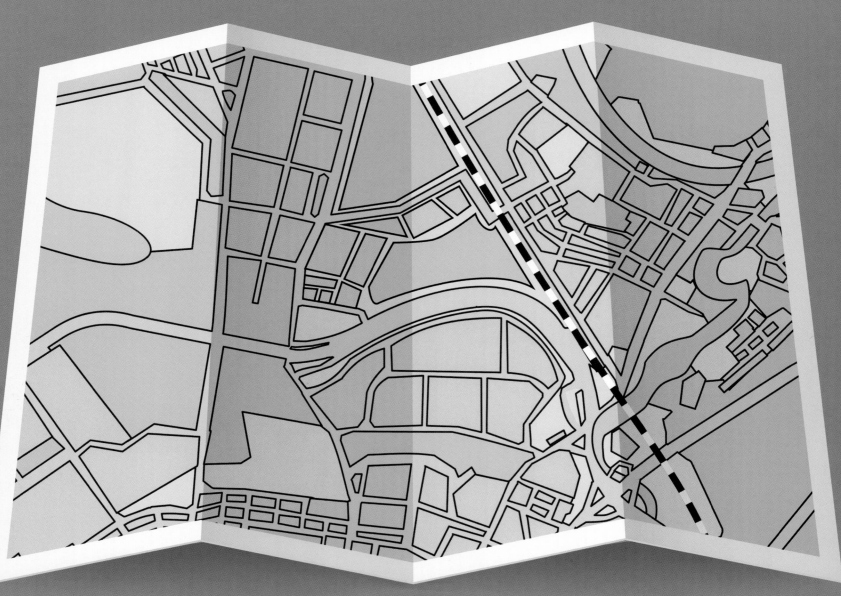

A map could be on paper or it could be digital. This means we look at it on a screen.

Digital Map

USING A MAP

Maps have different colours or symbols which represent places, buildings and services you can find.

This is a symbol you might see on a street map to show where a restaurant is.

Often, the symbols on a map look like the place they represent. You can also use a key, like this one, to check what the symbols mean.

HOUSE

DIRECTIONS

CAFÉ

PETROL

TELEPHONE

FOOD

Most maps are drawn from a 'bird's eye view'. This means that they show you how the area looks from above.

8

Each map usually has a **compass** printed on it, to show you which way on the map is north, south, east or west.

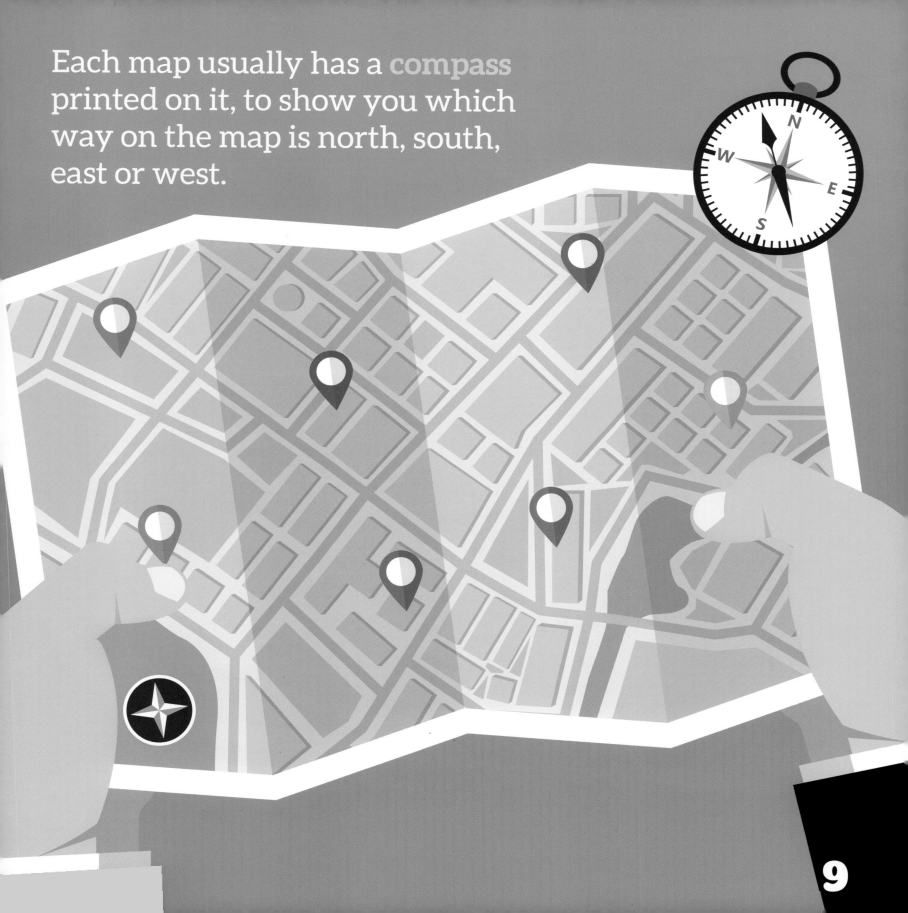

SCALE

Everything on a map has been made smaller, or 'scaled down' to fit.

The amount by which something is made smaller is called the scale.

A scale means we can use the map to show a long **distance** on a small map. If you want to know how long a road is, you can use the map scale.

1cm = 1 mile

STREET MAPS

A street map is a map which shows all the different streets in an area.

A street map might also show the different types of transport in that area.

STORE

STORE

Some street maps show us all the points of interest in an area too. These are places that people may find useful or interesting.

A restaurant is a point of interest.

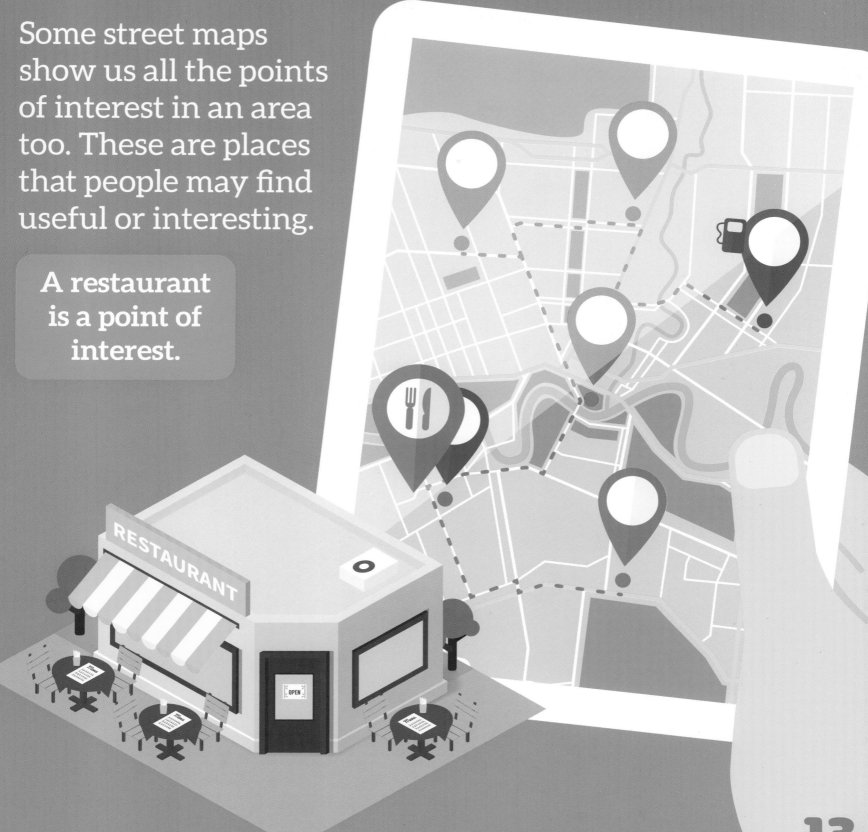

WHY MIGHT I USE A STREET MAP?

You could use a street map to help you find your way around your local area.

If you wanted to travel from your house to a nearby park but you didn't know the way, you could use a street map.

HOW IS A STREET MAP MADE?

To make a map, all the important information must be researched before you can start. For example: the locations of the points of interest.

What do you think these symbols mean?

Anyone can map their local area. All you need is paper, colouring pens and a ruler. Take an adult with you and explore your local area!

MAPPING MY AREA

CHOOSE YOUR AREA

Start by thinking about the area you would like to map.

DRAW THE ROADS

Draw the roads in the area you have chosen.

If you are drawing the road where you live, you could add other roads that come off it too.

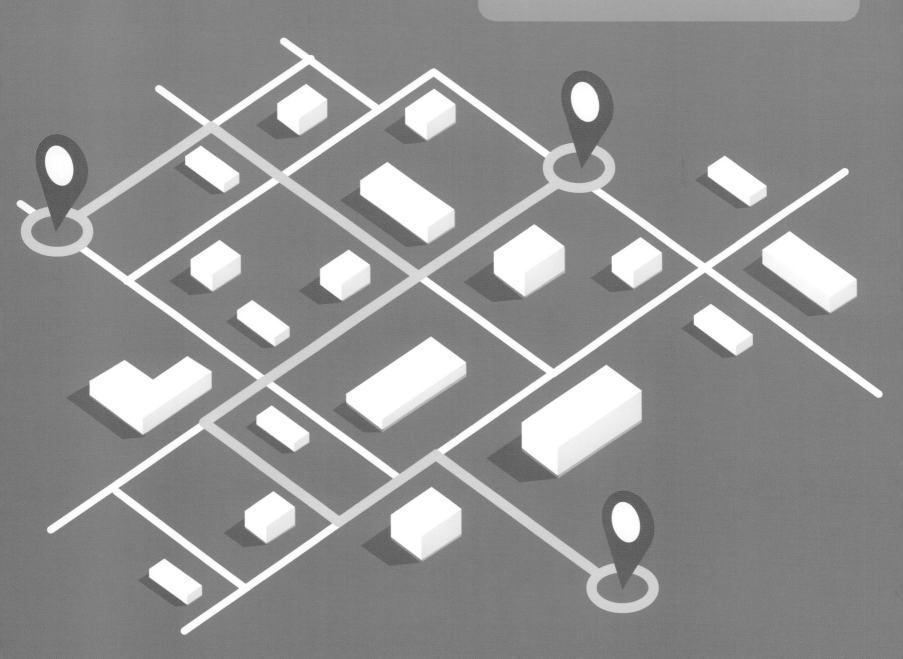

POINTS OF INTEREST

Make a list of any points of interest on your road. Is there a school or a shop nearby?

Colour them in to make your map clear and interesting.

CREATE A KEY

Create symbols for the points of interest and add them to the map in the correct place.

Then you can make a key.

ACTIVITY

CREATE A STREET MAP OF YOUR DREAM LOCATION

Create the street map of your dreams! Would you love to live next-door to a cinema? Or have a zoo in your garden?

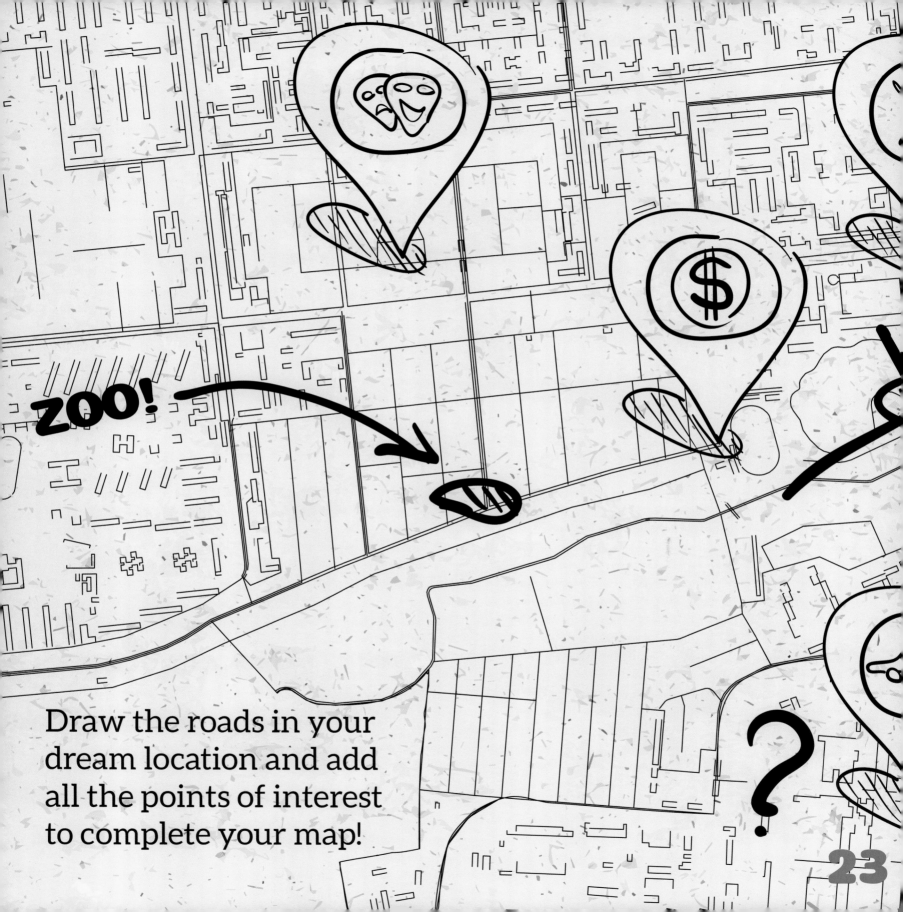

ZOO!

Draw the roads in your
dream location and add
all the points of interest
to complete your map!

23

GLOSSARY AND INDEX

GLOSSARY

area a specific place, for example land

compass a piece of equipment that can be used to show you north, south, east or west

distance the space between two points

locations particular places

population the number of things living in a particular place, for example people

represent to act on behalf of something else

researched to investigate or find information

symbols marks or pictures to show an object

transport carrying people or goods from one place to another using a vehicle, for example a train

INDEX